Blandford For
A Pictorial History

The north-east of the Market Place, *c.*1975

A PLAN of the Town

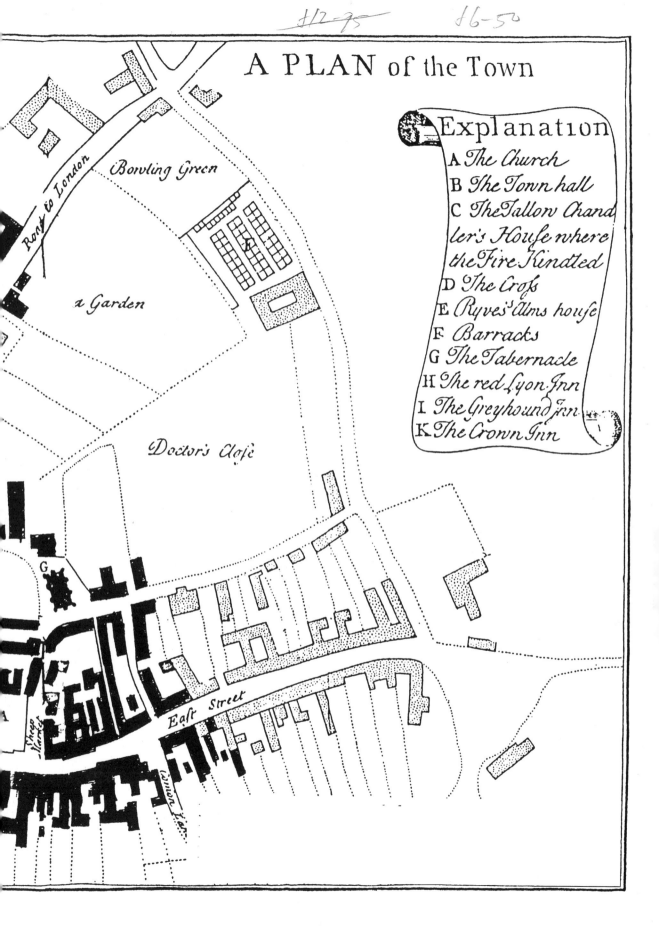

Road to London

Bowling Green

a Garden

Doctor's Close

East Street

Sheep Market

Church Lane

G

Explanation

A *The Church*
B *The Town hall*
C *The Tallow Chandler's House where the Fire Kindled*
D *The Cross*
E *Ryves' Alms house*
F *Barracks*
G *The Tabernacle*
H *The red Lyon Inn*
I *The Greyhound Inn*
K *The Crown Inn*

BLANDFORD FORUM

A Pictorial History

Ben Cox

Phillimore

1995

Published by
PHILLIMORE & CO. LTD.,
Shopwyke Manor Barn, Chichester, West Sussex

ISBN 0 85033 952 9

Printed and bound in Great Britain by
BIDDLES LTD.
Guildford, Surrey

List of Illustrations

Frontispiece: The north-east of the Market Place, *c.*1975

Acknowledgements

The majority of the photographs used in this work come from the collections held by the Blandford Forum Museum Trust, of which I am Honorary Curator, and my thanks are due to the Trust for permission to use them, and to those members of the public, too numerous to list here, who, over the years, presented them to the museum. Most of the older pictures are known to be the work of the Nesbitt and Hobbs families of Blandford who had photographic studios in the town between the 1860s and the 1920s. The remainder of the museum collections are the work of many local photographers of the past, whose identities cannot now be ascertained, but to whom I am indebted. I have also been able to select from the collections of Sam and Betty Jardine, who were in the photographic business here for many years, and from Dennis Waterman, a good friend of the museum, whose well-known collection of Blandford postcards was made available to me. Special thanks are due to the British Geographical Survey for the only known photograph of the Blandford Camp railway track, to Mr. D.E. Capewell, ARICS, for permission to use his railway photographs, to John Mosley and Joe Peaple for their generous contributions and to Jack Pountney for permission to use his drawing of Blandford before the fire. My manuscript has been expertly typed for transmission to my publisher by Anne Hosford, our museum secretary, and my very best thanks are due to her for carrying out this exacting task. Much valuable help has been given in dating pictures and putting names to faces by Blanfordians Charles Lavington, Charles Collier, Fred Gould, Leslie Bellows and Wyn and Monty Cox. Whilst every effort has been made to achieve accuracy, the old failing of not writing names, dates and places on the backs of photographs has made precise captioning difficult so I ask readers, please, to accept my apologies for any discrepancies which may have crept in.

Introduction

Early Days

There is no evidence of any substantial occupation in Blandford Forum in Romano-British times or earlier. At the time of the Norman Conquest nine separate units of Anglo-Saxon settlement existed near a major crossing of the river Stour a little east of the town's present river bridge. The area was known as Blaen-y-ford, meaning 'the place by the ford'. These settlements are all noted in the Domesday Survey of 1085-6 as either Bleneford or Blaneford. Not one of them was shown as having a church or to have attained urban status. They eventually formed themselves into groups according to their precise locations, to become the medieval parishes of Blandford Forum, Blandford St Mary, Blandford Brian (now Bryanston) and Langton Long Blandford. The Latin *Forum* was added to the group which became Blandford Forum to distinguish it from the other Blandfords and to indicate that it had become the market town for the area. The town expanded considerably over the centuries as it absorbed large parts of the parishes referred to above. The small 'd' in the middle of 'Blandford' appeared in the 16th century but many old Blandfordians still call the place 'Blaanverd'.

In 1106 Robert Duke of Normandy was defeated in battle by his younger brother, King Henry I, at Tinchebrai, a few miles from Mortain in the La Manche department of Normandy (now twinned with Blandford). Following this victory, Henry rewarded his close friend, chief minister and army commander, Robert de Beaumont, by creating him earl of Leicester, with the grant of estates in Dorset including what is now Blandford Forum. These estates were in addition to those given by William I to Robert's father, Roger de Beaumont, after 1066. From archives held by the Department of Eure in France I have ascertained that this Robert de Beaumont and his wife, Isabel, daughter of the king of France, founded the first church in what is now Blandford Forum, in about 1109. This was probably on the same site as the present church of St Peter and St Paul.

The last of the Beaumont lords of Blandford, also a Robert, died in 1204 without a male heir, but prior to his death he had given a large part of his Blandford estate to the Abbey of Dame Marie at Fontevrault in the Loire valley of France where King Henry II, his Queen Eleanor of Aquitaine and their son Richard I (*Coeur de Lion*) lie buried. This was the most favoured religious order of the royal and aristocratic families of England and Normandy. This separate manor became known as the Manor of Dame Marie, and the rents were payable to the abbey at Amesbury, towards the maintenance of the nuns of the Fontevrault order living there. We still have, on the eastern side of Blandford, the *Damory Arms*, Damory Street, Damory Court and the *Damory Oak* public house. During the ownership of this land by the Fontevrault order, the chapel and hospital of St Leonard was built. It was founded for the accommodation and care of lepers on land near where the parishes of Langton Long and Blandford Forum adjoined. The fourth Robert de Beaumont had been a crusader and also built the leper hospital of St Margaret at Pamphill near Wimborne. Both foundations were on his estates, and each had been built as an act of Christian charity influenced, no doubt, by the fact that one of his brothers, William, had contracted leprosy whilst away on crusade, and may well have been cared for in one of them. The present chapel, the only medieval building in Blandford, was built in the late 14th or early 15th century on the site of the original chapel. In early Victorian times the chapel, hospital and ancillary buildings were more or less derelict and were converted to agricultural use. The chapel was extended east and west and became the middle section of a barn. These extensions have recently been removed and work is in progress to restore the chapel, as far as possible, to its original state. Although the other buildings were clearly shown on the 1902 Ordnance Survey map, they were subsequently demolished.

After the defeat and death of Simon de Montfort, earl of Leicester, at the battle of Evesham in 1265, his estates in Dorset, including those at Blandford, were seized by the king and granted to the de Lacy family, earls of Lincoln. The de Lacys line was ended through lack of male heirs and the estates passed to Henry Bolingbroke, Duke of Lancaster who, in 1399, became Henry IV. The town then became a parcel of the Duchy of Lancaster and remained so until 1605.

By the 17th century the principal landowners at Blandford were the Ryves family of Damory Court, Blandford, and the Portman family who in the 1660s acquired the Bryanston estate west of the town from the Rogers, who had been there since 1415. The Ryves family subsequently sold off their Damory lands and residence and went to live at their more secluded seat at Ranston a few miles away. The Portman family was to have an enormous influence upon local affairs as the estates grew to something like 7,000 acres and included much of the town. Edward Berkeley Portman (1799-1888) became the 1st Viscount Portman and was married to Emma Lascelles, daughter of the earl of Harewood. After the death of the 3rd Viscount in 1923 the family decided to sell their mansion house which became Bryanston public school in 1927. By 1950 the remainder of the Bryanston estate had found its way via the Exchequer into the hands of the commissioners for crown lands, in discharge of the heavy burden of estate duty arising on the deaths of the 5th, 6th and 7th Viscounts Portman during the 1940s.

The Economy

From medieval times Blandford Forum has been primarily dependent upon farming. The main crops grown on the surrounding chalk Downlands were wheat and barley, and these were dependent upon the folding of vast flocks of sheep which were sold in the town's markets and fairs. These markets were also popular for the sale of cattle, horses and dairy produce from the valleys of the river Stour, the Tarrant and Winterbourne brooks. Soon after the town became established as a market it was necessary to stimulate trade by the erection of a bridge over the Stour to take traffic into and out of the town from the Dorchester direction. There had previously been times when traffic could not negotiate the ancient fording place to the east. This bridge is first documented in 1278 as 'pons de Blaneford' but may well have been there many years earlier. The town's markets were originally held on a Sunday, partly in the parish church. When King John visited Blandford in 1214 he ordered that the weekly markets should thereafter be held on Saturdays, as they still are.

The fairs originally held in the town took place at the times of religious festivals and are first recorded in 1279. They were mainly there for the sale and purchase of livestock, cheese, wool, horses and cattle, but there was also much dancing and singing, entertainment by strolling players who went from fair to fair, meetings of friends and relatives and the dissemination of news. Later these fairs, usually held four or six times a year, lasted for two or three days but sometimes longer. This basic agricultural economy was supplemented, following the suppression of the Dorset monasteries, when further prosperity was engendered by the many large country houses which were built in the district on former abbey lands. These provided the Blandford area with a new class of wealthy merchants, diplomats, Members of Parliament and others wishing to become country landowners. Their estate farms provided much of the livestock upon which Blandford depended for its markets and fairs. Those living on these new estates, now our local villages, came into the town for the services and goods not obtainable where they lived.

The Market Cross at the west end of the Market Place survived the Great Fire of 1731 but was subsequently removed as it was deemed to be a hindrance to traffic. The borough council met many times to consider rebuilding it in a more convenient place but nothing came of their deliberations. Is it now too late? It was described as 'the place where traders exposed for sale pig meat, pastry-cook goods, cheese and bacon', the sales being mostly conducted by women who brought their produce in from the villages. Until the main street shops gradually came into being in the 18th century, the street markets were the principal outlets for the Blandford traders and nearly everything in the way of food, clothes, shoes, ironmongery and general necessities could be bought there. In the 1820s the livestock markets were moved out of the Market Place to the smaller market places on Sheep Market Hill, the Tabernacle and the Outhayes. It is believed that the moves took place because the well-to-do merchants residing in the Market Place were greatly troubled by the noise and smells emanating from the markets. The fairs were moved out of the town completely, into a field off the Salisbury road which became known as 'The Fairfield'. It is now built on, being the area between Fairfield Road and Castleman House, the site of the former Union Workhouse. The fairs continued there until the 1940s but by then were little more than livestock sales.

There was very little long-distance vehicular traffic in medieval times and this put considerable restrictions on trade between towns. By the 16th century this situation was slowly being remedied and as more use was made of vehicles for carrying goods and people, so the roads improved and in turn trade increased. By the end of the 17th century there was a fairly well-organised and growing traffic between towns—the coaching era had begun. Blandford was fortunate in being able to take advantage of the fact that it was on the main London to Exeter route and a convenient halfway stopping place. The town's main inns, the *Crown*, the *Greyhound*, the *Red Lion* and the *Bell* underwent considerable enlargement to cope with the greater volume of travellers, their vehicles and horses. For two hundred years or so this coaching trade was a very welcome 'extra' to the town's economy, providing as it did employment for ostlers, grooms, cooks, maids, butchers, coachbuilders, farriers and others required to meet the needs of the travellers. The oldest of these inns was the *Crown* which has been on the same site at least since 1465. When the railway came to the town in the 1860s this coaching trade came to a rapid end. Many people lost their jobs and much of the hotel accommodation was taken over for other purposes.

In addition to its agricultural economy and the coaching trade Blandford had all the usual tinkers, tailors, butchers, bakers and other tradesmen usually found in towns. However there were others of major importance, particularly those engaged in the wool trade; those dealing in wool at Blandford were mostly wool staplers who processed wool before despatching it to the clothing manufacturers. The principal wool staplers at Blandford were for generations members of the Barnes family who were mayors of the town on many occasions, and great benefactors.

From the 17th century Blandford had become quite well-known for its cottage-based buttonmaking industry controlled by one or two factors who supplied the materials and sold the finished work. This all came to an end following the Great Exhibition of 1851 where John Ashton exhibited his buttonmaking machine. Blandford was, however, pretty resilient and most of these workers went on to do gloving and straw-plaiting.

For over two hundred years Blandford has been famous for its brewing industry. Until the 18th century innkeepers and estate owners generally brewed their own ales and beers, but in later years they began to sell their products to other inns. One of these was George Cross who had premises in White Cliff Mill Street (now the White Cliff Nursing Home). In the 1731 fire at Blandford he lost his brewhouses, his chambers above and two dwellings on this site. In the 1770s the rebuilt premises were occupied by brewer William Clapcott. He was described as a 'beer and porter brewer' and also had another brewery over the river at Blandford St Mary. This business later passed through various owners including the Hector family, and ultimately to Hall & Woodhouse Ltd., the present owners, as an addition to their Ansty brewery. The premises are now very much enlarged and the company is now the largest employer in the district, other than the Ministry of Defence at Blandford camp.

The Great Fire of Blandford, 1731

As Blandford was never the site of a Roman villa, a great abbey, castle or battlefield, the Great Fire of 4 June 1731 must be regarded as the major event in the town's history. The seat of the fire was a soap-boiler's premises on the site now occupied by the *King's Arms*. The inferno destroyed the parish church, the town grammar school, the Town Hall and all but a dozen of the town's houses, public buildings, inns and business premises. Parts of Blandford St Mary and Bryanston over the river were also destroyed. Properties not destroyed included the Old House in The Close, the Ryves Almshouses, Dale House and other buildings at the upper ends of Salisbury Street and White Cliff Mill Street, and several between Stour House and the end of East Street. The fire effectively hastened the end of an epidemic of smallpox that had been raging in Blandford at the time. The parish registers show only 12 people 'burnt and interred' on 4 June. The cost of rebuilding the town was provided by private donations, including £1,000 from George II, £200 from Queen Caroline, £100 from the Prince of Wales and varying amounts from peers, commoners, universities, churches, towns and cities throughout the country. Old Blandfordian Willliam Wake, then Archbishop of Canterbury, gave £100, and Drury Lane Theatre put on a play 'for the unhappy sufferers from the late fire'. The spending of the money was controlled by commissioners appointed by the Crown under the authority of a special Act of Parliament. The bulk of the rebuilding was carried out under the supervision of local master builders John and William Bastard who did much of the work themselves and employed numerous subcontractors. They were, in fact, Blandford's first town-planners and ensured that many obstructions and bottlenecks in the streets were removed for the better movement of traffic, and maximum space for use as the principal market place. Central Blandford is today very much as it was rebuilt after the fire, with very few 'then and now' photographic opportunities. One has to date pictures as near as possible from any vehicles shown or the clothing of people appearing in them. After the fire, the town quickly recovered its economy, the coaching inns were rebuilt and enlarged, and the markets and fairs continued as usual almost without a break. A temporary church was built in what was then called Winchester Square but has since been known as The Tabernacle. It was all very traumatic for the people of Blandford at the time, but they must have been thankful it all happened during the daytime and in midsummer. By 1760 the town was regarded as having been rebuilt, the event being marked by the erection of a monument in the Market Place. This catastrophe has, however, left us with one of the finest Georgian town centres in England, fully protected by strictly enforced conservation orders.

Local Government

In 1399 Blandford Forum became a parcel of the Duchy of Lancaster, and a steward was appointed to oversee local affairs, to protect Duchy interests and to collect such dues as were payable. This arrangement continued until 1605 when James I granted the town its first Charter of Incorporation. The intention of this, and many other charters issued by him at this time, was to bring some uniformity into local government for the benefit of the public at large and to bring to an end corrupt practices. It confirmed most of the town's old privileges and customs and recited that it would result in 'the better government, rule and bettering of the said borough'. The charter did not however confer upon the borough the right to have its own magistracy, nor to send members to parliament. This form of government continued successfully until 1835 when many of the borough's powers were curtailed by the passing of the Municipal Corporations Act. This act did however order that the town should be run by a mayor, aldermen and councillors, and that they should all be elected by those people in the town entitled to vote. Further powers were lost following the coming of county councils in 1888 and rural district councils in 1894. By the Local Government Act of 1973 the town lost its borough status and is now administered by the Blandford Forum Town Council who endeavour to keep up many of the old traditions associated with the former borough.

Churches and Chapels

The present parish church of St Peter and St Paul was rebuilt between 1731 and 1739 on the site of the earlier medieval church, completely destroyed in the 1731 fire. The work was carried out under the control of John and William Bastard but funds ran out and they could not complete the work to their entire satisfaction; the proposed tower and steeple could not be started, and no provision was made for a proper chancel and choir. Nevertheless they produced what is universally recognised as the most pleasing Georgian church in the baroque style outside London. The tower was added after 1739 and topped by a cupola which still stands, although described by the Bastard brothers at the time as a 'temporary wooden structure' with which they would not be associated. It is still in place, and in keeping with its surroundings. The lack of a chancel was remedied in 1895 when, by the use of jacks and rollers, the apsidal east end was moved from its original position some thirty feet further east on new foundations, to provide room for choir stalls and chancel. The interior is beautiful and much in the style of the London 'Wren' churches. Of special interest are the handsomely carved chair made in 1748 for the bailiffs of Blandford, and the magnificent organ in the west end gallery which was designed for the Chapel Royal, Savoy, but proved too large. The crown and the Prince of Wales' feathers remained as part of the decoration. The former galleries to the north and south were removed in recent years.

The first Dissenters' chapel in Blandford appeared soon after the Restoration of the monarchy in 1660 when the rector of Blandford, William Alleine, unwilling to comply with the provisions of the Act of Uniformity which followed, resigned his living. Then, with a considerable following he formed his own congregation of dissenting Protestants and became their minister; the services were held in Longhorne's barn, between Salisbury Street and White Cliff Mill Street. A new meeting house was erected there in 1722 but only lasted nine years as it was destroyed in the 1731 fire. The new chapel which replaced it was Congregational, and was itself replaced in 1867 by the present building which is now the United Reformed Church.

The Wesleyan Methodists were active in Blandford during the time of John Wesley's ministry—his grandfather had been gaoled in Blandford for nonconformity, but in 1672 he was granted a licence to hold services in the town. The community's first chapel was erected in The Close in 1834. It was enlarged in 1874 and schoolrooms were added in 1905. The Primitive Methodists formed their separate chapel which was erected in Albert Street in 1877. They united with the Wesleyans in 1932, but continued to hold separate services until 1976 when the premises were taken over by the Blandford Evangelical Church which still enjoys good congregations there.

The Roman Catholics had their first church erected along the Milldown Road in 1934, dedicating it to Our Lady of Lourdes and St Cecilia. Previously the Blandford and district Catholics met for many years at the convent of St Monica at nearby Spetisbury and after this was closed in 1927, at various Catholic homes including The Old House in The Close at Blandford.

Education

Blandford has a fine record as regards the provision of education from medieval times to the present day. The first school of which records exist was the borough's Free Grammar School. A date for its original foundation has not yet been ascertained, but the borough chamberlain's accounts for 1653-4 record expenditure on repairs to the property which was just north of the parish churchyard. Among those who had their early schooling here was John Aubrey (1626-97), the distinguished historian and biographer, who described the establishment as 'the most eminent school for the education of gentlemen in the West of England'. This was no idle boast as other boys who distinguished themselves were William Wake (1657-1736), who became Archbishop of Canterbury; Bruno Ryves (1596-1677), chaplain to Charles I and Charles II and Dean of Windsor; Robert Frampton (1622-1677), Bishop of Gloucester; Thomas Creech (1659-1700), translator of Lucretius, Horace, Virgil and others; Samuel Lisle (1683-1749), Bishop of Norwich; Walter Blandford who became Bishop of Worcester in 1671 and Thomas Lindsay (1655-1724), son of the rector of Blandford, who became Archbishop of Armagh and Primate of all Ireland. What a record for a small country town!

William Wake did not forget his early schooling days in Blandford for in his will he provided trust funds for the education of 12 poor boys of the town and stipulated that they be clothed in the manner of the London Bluecoat Schools. No provision was made for a school building and the boys had to be taught in the homes of self-employed schoolmasters. Although Wake died in 1736 the scheme did not get started until 1757 owing to the difficulty in getting trustees willing to act, but eventually the borough council took over responsibility. The masters were paid one pound per annum for each of the 12 boys, their clothing was provided as directed and their apprenticeships paid for. In the 1840s when the National School became established in Park Road, the boys went there and received the same education as the other town children did. By 1939 admissions had ceased as the boys were refusing to wear the uniform of tam-o'-shanter cap, black or blue gown, knee breeches, yellow stockings etc. and their parents did not like them to be known as 'charity boys'.

The Milton Abbey Grammar School moved to Blandford from nearby Milton Abbas in 1752 and was for many years in competition with the Borough Grammar School, causing the latter to close in 1834 when the premises were sold by the borough to provide funds for a new market house.

The Milldown Endowed School was founded in 1862 by Thomas Horlock Bastard of Charlton Marshall and erected on land between Damory Street and Salisbury Road. After a few setbacks the governors got it going on the right lines, and by 1903 it had become the Blandford Secondary School. It was further improved in 1928 when, following the closure of the Milton Abbey Grammar School in Blandford on its move to Whatcombe, it became the Blandford Grammar School. In 1968 it went 'comprehensive' and moved to new premises in the Bryanston deer park.

The town had many, mostly short-lived 'dame' schools and academies, a British School from 1848 in White Cliff Mill Street for the children of nonconformist families and a 'ragged' school in Bryanston Street which opened on Sundays in the Mission Room provided by the Portman family. Over the years Blandford has been well served with schools, as it is today. Many of the big country houses within a few miles of Blandford are also now occupied as public schools, the nearest being Bryanston.

Social Life

With the improved conditions and educational advances of the mid-19th century, the working classes were gradually able to participate in social activities previously not available to them. Most continued to seek their entertainment and social activity either in the public houses or at their churches or chapels. The town had its cricket team as early as 1834, as well as its football teams of much earlier origin. Bowls was played here in the 17th century and fishing was always popular. The first public library opened in 1833 in the Grand Assembly Rooms in West Street, which was doubling as the venue for concerts, balls and public meetings before the town's Corn Exchange become more popular for these occasions, and as a further education centre.

The first cinema, the Picture Palace, opened in East Street soon after the First World War. It was improved and enlarged in 1927 and continued to serve the town until a new Palace was erected on the opposite side of the road. During the Second World War, due to the great influx of service people, it was found necessary to re-open the original Picture Palace which then became The Ritz. The Ritz finally closed its doors in 1957 leaving the Palace (at present Gateways) to survive as a cinema for a few more years into the 1960s. Many look back with pleasure to the annual shows staged at the Palace by the local Footlight Follies, and the Corn Exchange performances of the Choral Society, the Operatic and Dramatic Society, the Town Band and others. The annual street carnival has continued from time immemorial and is still a much favoured annual event. Since 1960 the town has been fortunate in having, as near as Bryanston, the Arts Centre which provides first-class musical and dramatic entertainment by well-known performers and musicians.

The Changing Scene

The Victorian era saw more improvements providing a better quality of life than ever before. The town was first lit by gas in 1837; the Corn Exchange was built in 1858 replacing the earlier Market House behind the Town Hall. A new union workhouse was built in Salisbury Road in 1859. The telephone came in the 1880s via the National Telephone Company, and the cottage hospital was founded for the town and district in 1888 by Viscountess Portman and the Hon. L.E. Portman. This was but one of the many charitable foundations and benefits provided by the Portman family.

The coming of the railway to Blandford was probably the major event of the Victorian era. The Dorset Central line, which was planned to run from Wimborne to Blandford, was opened to traffic on 1 October 1860 but terminated at Blandford St Mary. As the Somerset Central Railway was also planning a route to Blandford at this time, negotiations between the two companies resulted in the formation of the Somerset & Dorset Joint Railway. Bridges were erected over the Stour and at the Damory end of East Street, with a new station in Blandford Forum.

The coming of the pedal cycle, which enabled the keen club cyclist to travel up to 100 miles a day, was a great boon for some, as was the coming of the motor car but these forms of travel had little effect on the railway services which continued until the line was closed to passenger traffic in March 1966 and for freight in February 1967. From people who were in business in the town at the time, I gather the loss of the goods traffic was felt the most.

Although the site of Blandford camp has been in use on and off for some 200 years, mostly for militia and yeomanry training, it was little used between 1923 and 1939. In 1939 it was re-opened for the training of conscripts and other branches of the military. It was greatly enlarged in 1943 to provide the 22nd United States military hospital which was to take casualties from the second front in Europe, most of whom came by air ambulances via the nearby Tarrant Rushton airfield which played such a big part in the events of D-Day in June 1944. During the Second World War the town of Blandford was created an anti-tank 'island' protected by the river Stour, the railway embankments, anti-tank ditches, large numbers of concrete 'dragons' teeth', pill-boxes and other installations designed to hold up any enemy invasion. Many of these can still be seen in different parts of the town.

Since the war the Blandford military camp has grown in size and importance as the principal depot of the Royal Corps of Signals. The soldiers, their families and the many civilian workers employed there enjoy a very good relationship with the people of Blandford and contribute greatly to the town's economy. Other modern developments include the creation of large industrial estates north of the town and a great extension of the housing programme concentrated in the Milldown area.

Fortunately the town's Georgian centre is jealously guarded and protected by its current conservation restrictions, ensuring its continuance as one of the most attractive country towns in Dorset, famed for its architecture, riverscape, shopping facilities and its friendly people. Many of the gaps in this introduction will be filled on reference to the pictures I have selected, and the captions to them—every picture tells a story, they say.

Pre-1900

1   Blandford artist Mr. J.D. Pountney's impression, based on the known facts and plans, shows the town's Market Place much as it was in the 17th century.

2 Thomas Lindsay (1655-1724), Archbishop of Armagh and Primate of all Ireland in 1715. He was the son of the rector of Blandford and attended the town's grammar school.

3 Dr. William Wake (1657-1736), Blandford-born son of Colonel William Wake—a soldier in the Civil War. Dr. Wake became Archbishop of Canterbury in 1715 and by his will provided trust funds for the establishment of the Blandford Bluecoat School.

4 The Ryves Almshouses in Salisbury Street founded in 1682 by George Ryves of Damory Court during his term of office as county sheriff. The property survived the great fire of 1731.

5 Badge which all occupiers of the Ryves Almshouses were obliged to wear when not in their houses. The obligation was discontinued c.1850.

6 The Old House in The Close built *c*.1625 for German Protestant refugees from Bohemia settling in Blandford following the removal of their king and queen in 1619. The western end of the house was damaged by the fire of 1731.

7 Dale House in Salisbury Street was another of the pre-fire houses to escape destruction. The front seen here was rebuilt shortly after the fire. It is now the Constitution Club.

8 (*right*) John (1689-1770) and (*below*) William (1690-1766) Bastard, the Blandford builders and architects who undertook supervision of the rebuilding of Blandford after the 1731 fire. Their portraits hang in Blandford Town Hall.

9 Coupar House in Church Street is probably the finest of the post-fire houses built by the Bastard brothers. It was at one time home of the famous botanist Dr. Richard Pultney (1730-1801) and later of Francis James Stuart, 16th Earl of Moray (1842-1909). He owned three castles, two mansions, and about 81,000 acres of land in Scotland. It is now the headquarters of the Blandford Royal British Legion.

10 Engraving of the famous Damory oak in 1747. The oak stood at the east end of the town and served as an inn capable of holding 200 occupants. It had a 68 ft. circumference, and the interior was 15ft. wide and 17 ft. high. It was sold standing for £14 in 1755 and felled for firewood.

A

CATALOGUE

OF THE

moſt Uſeful & Ornamental

HARDY TREES,

Shrubs, Plants, &c.

ALSO OF THE

Herbaceous Plants, Fruit-Trees, Garden Seeds, Flower Roots, Flowering Shrubs, &c.

SOLD BY

JOHN KINGSTON GALPINE
Nurſery and Seedſman,

AT BLANDFORD,

D O R S E T,

Where Catalogues may be had, Price Six-Pence.

BLANDFORD : Printed by S. SIMMONDS, M,DCC,LXXXII.

11 The 1782 catalogue of Blandford nurseryman John Kingston Galpine. This is the oldest of such catalogues to have been found in the West Country. Galpine was a gentleman nurseryman of good family who provided for the many country houses in the Blandford area.

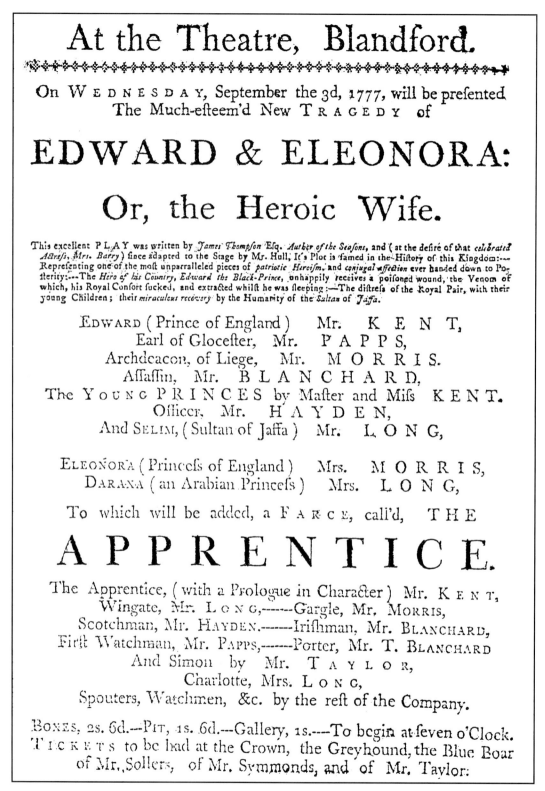

At the Theatre, Blandford.

On WEDNESDAY, September the 3d, 1777, will be presented
The Much-esteem'd New TRAGEDY of

EDWARD & ELEONORA:

Or, the Heroic Wife.

This excellent PLAY was written by *James Thompson* Esq. *Author of the Seasons*, and (at the desire of that *celebrated Actress, Mrs. Barry*) since adapted to the Stage by Mr. Hull, It's Plot is famed in the History of this Kingdom:—Representing one of the most unparalleled pieces of *patriotic Heroism,* and *conjugal affection* ever handed down to Posterity:—The Hero of his Country, *Edward the Black-Prince,* unhappily receives a poisoned wound, the Venom of which, his Royal Consort sucked, and extracted whilst he was sleeping:—The distress of the Royal Pair, with their young Children; their *miraculous recovery* by the Humanity of the *Sultan of Jaffa.*

EDWARD (Prince of England)   Mr. KENT,
Earl of Glocester, Mr. PAPPS,
Archdeacon, of Liege, Mr. MORRIS.
Assassin, Mr. BLANCHARD,
The YOUNG PRINCES by Master and Miss KENT.
Officer, Mr. HAYDEN,
And SELIM, (Sultan of Jaffa) Mr. LONG,

ELEONORA (Princess of England) Mrs. MORRIS,
DARAXA (an Arabian Princess) Mrs. LONG,

To which will be added, a FARCE, call'd, THE

APPRENTICE.

The Apprentice, (with a Prologue in Character) Mr. KENT,
Wingate, Mr. LONG,——Gargle, Mr. MORRIS,
Scotchman, Mr. HAYDEN.——Irishman, Mr. BLANCHARD,
First Watchman, Mr. PAPPS,——Porter, Mr. T. BLANCHARD
And Simon by Mr. TAYLOR,
Charlotte, Mrs. LONG,
Spouters, Watchmen, &c. by the rest of the Company.

BOXES, 2s. 6d.---PIT, 1s. 6d.---Gallery, 1s.----To begin at seven o'Clock.
TICKETS to be had at the Crown, the Greyhound, the Blue Boar
of Mr. Sollers, of Mr. Symmonds, and of Mr. Taylor:

12 Theatre bill of 1777 found recently in the roof of premises in White Cliff Mill Street, now part of the White Cliff Nursing Home.

13 The Grand Assembly Rooms in West Street were built in 1772. Concerts, balls, meetings, lectures and many other activities took place there. The building can be seen on the right of this picture (taken from the bridge). The premises are now used for business.

14 Ticket for a concert at the Assembly Rooms in 1794. Famous singers and musicians performed at these concerts especially during Blandford's annual race week.

CONCERT.

Blandford   Affembly-Rooms,

Wednefday Evening,   October 15, 1794.

15 Extract from Robert Morden's map of Dorset made before the Great Fire of 1731 and showing the London Road then in use passing through Cranborne.

16 The former town Grammar School as rebuilt after the 1731 fire. In the 19th century it became Blandford's first savings bank and is now called Bank House.

17 Engraving of the east end of Blandford Market Place *c.*1800 showing the fire pump of 1760, the church of St Peter and St Paul, the Bastard memorial in the churchyard and, at the back, part of the town's grammar school.

18 The original Wesleyan Chapel in The Close built in 1834—it was greatly enlarged to the west in later years to provide Sunday school rooms and other amenities.

19 Notice of the removal of the sheep fair from the town to a field in the Salisbury Road in 1822. The new site was between the railway line and the present Castleman House.

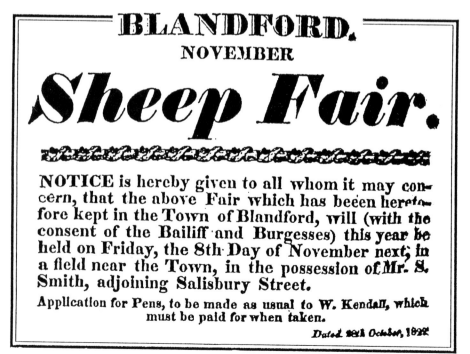

BLANDFORD.
NOVEMBER
Sheep Fair.

NOTICE is hereby given to all whom it may concern, that the above Fair which has beéen heretofore kept in the Town of Blandford, will (with the consent of the Bailiff and Burgesses) this year be held on Friday, the 8th Day of November next, in a field near the Town, in the possession of Mr. S. Smith, adjoining Salisbury Street.

Application for Pens, to be made as usual to W. Kendall, which must be paid for when taken.

Dated 28th October, 1822.

BLANDFORD
GAS AND COKE
COMPANY.

The Inhabitants of Blandford who intend lighting their Shops, Houses, or other Establishments, with Gas, are respectfully requested to intimate their intentions at the Gas-Office, or to give their orders for Service Pipes when called on for that purpose by the Foreman of the works, in order that the men may be enabled during the progress of the works, to lay the communication with the main pipes in the most advantageous manner, that any unnecessary expense to the consumers of Gas and the Company may be avoided.

The attention of the Inhabitants is likewise called to the necessity of their giving an early order for interior fittings; the Company thinking it right to advise the consumers to make early preparations for their supply of light, as they fully expect to be able to supply Gas by the time contracted for.

By order of the Committee,

JOHN SHIPP,

Honorary Secretary.

Blandford, Dec. 5th. 1836.

SHIPP, PRINTER, BLANDFORD

20 An 1836 invitation to the people of Blandford to become consumers of gas from the new gas works of the Blandford Gas & Coke Company.

21 (*above*) Engraving of Blandford Market Place made in the 1830s for presentation to Edward Berkeley Portman on his elevation to the peerage as Baron Portman. In 1873 he was created Viscount Portman of Bryanston.

22 (*left*) Alfred Stevens (1818-75), a self-portrait of 1832. Born in Blandford, he became famous as a designer, sculptor and artist and was often described as 'the English Michelangelo'. He designed the memorial to the Duke of Wellington in St Paul's Cathedral and the ornate floor in St George's, Liverpool. (Courtesy of the Tate Gallery who house the bulk of Stevens' works.)

23 (*right*) William and Thomas Hammond's advertisement of *c.*1855. They carried goods to the nearest railway station before the line came to Blandford in the 1860s.

WILLIAM AND THOMAS HAMMOND,
GENERAL RAILWAY CARRIERS,
BLANDFORD.

——

To LONDON, and all other PARTS.

——

LONDON OFFICES.
NAG'S HEAD BOROUGH, and 20 OLD CHANGE.

Goods sent into either the above Offices before 5 o'Clock
will be delivered at Vauxhall Station the same Night.

HENVILLE, PRINTER BLANDFORD.

24 The interior of the church of St Peter and St Paul about 1875, showing the apsidal east end with pulpit but no chancel or choir stalls. These nave galleries were removed in 1971.

25 The organ in the west gallery of the parish church erected in 1794—it had been intended for the Chapel Royal, Savoy, but proved too large and was bought by Blandford for £500 11s. 0d.

26 The church was extended to the east by 30 ft. in 1895 to provide a proper chancel and choir stalls. Here is the work in progress.

FUNERAL

OF HIS

Late Majesty,

WILLIAM IV.

As the time of the Funeral of our late lamented Sovereign is fixed for Saturday the 8th. of July, it is considered to be extremely inconvenient to the Inhabitants of this Town to observe the whole of that day, (being the Market day), with all that solemnity and respect which their loyalty would dictate.

With the advice of many Members of the Town Council, I therefore recommend that at 6 o'Clock in the Evening of that day, the Shops should be closed, the business of the Market terminated, and the remainder of the day observed with all the decorum such an event demands.

HENRY ABBOTT,

Mayor.

Blandford, July 1st. 1837.

SHIPP, PRINTER, BLANDFORD.

27 1837 notice concerning the arrangements for the funeral of William IV.

28 The new union workhouse erected in Salisbury Road in 1858 on land given by Viscount Portman.

29 Smart & Son's carnival float of *c.*1895 being towed by one of their steam traction engines.

30 The new Bryanston House which was completed for the Portman family in the 1890s. The family gave up occupation in the 1920s and the house is now Bryanston public school.

31 Tne main entrance lodge to the Portman estate near Blandford bridge, *c*.1920.

32 Langton House, built in 1827-30, on the site of an earlier house for the Farquharson family. The house was occupied by soldiers during the Second World War and was demolished in 1949.

33 James John Farquharson, squire of Langton. He was very famous as a Master of Foxhounds. He was also founder of the Blandford Independent Troop of Yeomanry Cavalry and was its commanding officer from 1831-38 when the troop was disbanded. He died in 1871. This portrait is in Dorchester museum.

34 Blandford's first National School, *c*.1840. It is now the Archbishop Wake first school. The premises in Park Road are much as originally built.

35 The main entrance to Blandford's United Reformed Church built in 1866 as a replacement of the one built after the 1731 fire.

36 (*right*) Meeting in the Crown meadow of branches of the Ancient Order of Free Foresters, *c.*1906.

37 (*below left*) The south side of the Market Place in 1901 on the occasion of the coronation of King Edward VII.

38 (*below right*) Alfred Dean, grocer and postmaster in Albert Street, out delivering at nearby Turnworth, *c.*1900.

39 Brewery cottages at Blandford St Mary built in 1872 but recently demolished. The unusual use of brick work is of special interest. The 'spade' design is unexplained.

40 Hall & Woodhouse's new brewery, designed by Arthur Kinder & Co., and completed in 1900.

41 Durden's Corner at the west end of the Market Place, *c*.1895. Many of the adjoining premises had still not been converted to shops.

42 Brass memorial to George Vince in the parish church. Vince's parents had a fish shop in West Street and he had been a pupil at the town's Bluecoat School. It took over a year for the news of his death to reach the Admiralty. (Photograph courtesy of John Mosley.)

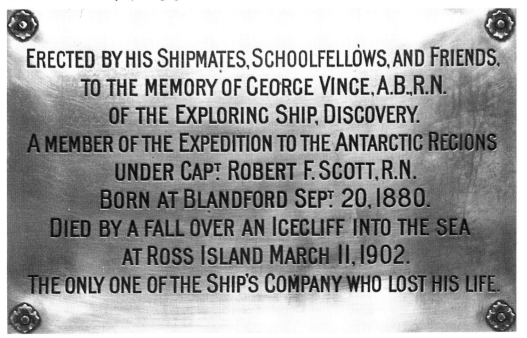

ERECTED BY HIS SHIPMATES, SCHOOLFELLOWS, AND FRIENDS,
TO THE MEMORY OF GEORGE VINCE, A.B., R.N.
OF THE EXPLORING SHIP, DISCOVERY.
A MEMBER OF THE EXPEDITION TO THE ANTARCTIC REGIONS
UNDER CAP.T ROBERT F. SCOTT, R.N.
BORN AT BLANDFORD SEP.T 20, 1880.
DIED BY A FALL OVER AN ICECLIFF INTO THE SEA
AT ROSS ISLAND MARCH 11, 1902.
THE ONLY ONE OF THE SHIP'S COMPANY WHO LOST HIS LIFE.

43 Blandford cyclists with the latest in men's 'safety' cycles, *c.*1897.

44 The end of Victoria's glorious reign. Notice of general mourning arrangements for Blandford in 1901.

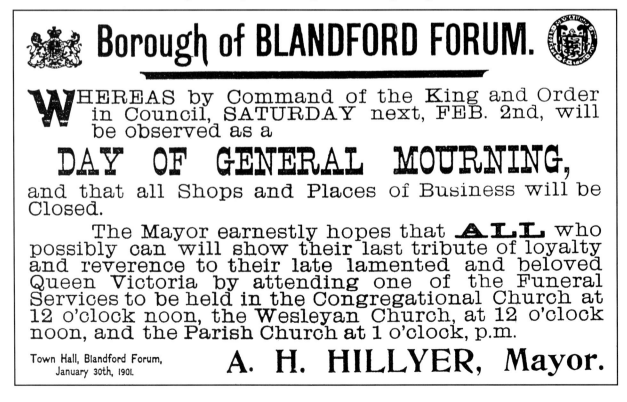

Borough of BLANDFORD FORUM.

WHEREAS by Command of the King and Order in Council, SATURDAY next, FEB. 2nd, will be observed as a

DAY OF GENERAL MOURNING,

and that all Shops and Places of Business will be Closed.

The Mayor earnestly hopes that **ALL** who possibly can will show their last tribute of loyalty and reverence to their late lamented and beloved Queen Victoria by attending one of the Funeral Services to be held in the Congregational Church at 12 o'clock noon, the Wesleyan Church, at 12 o'clock noon, and the Parish Church at 1 o'clock, p.m.

Town Hall, Blandford Forum,
January 30th, 1901.

A. H. HILLYER, Mayor.

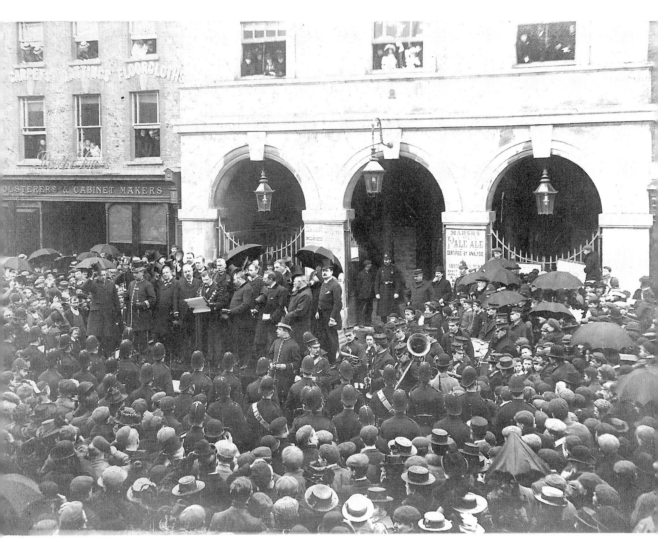

45　Proclamation of King Edward VII being read outside the Town Hall by the Mayor, Albert H. Hillyer, 1901.

*c.*1900-1920

46   The *Blandford Express* newspaper office snowed under in 1891. The paper was published from 1869-1894.

47 Charming Blandford greetings card of 1901 produced by Blandford printers T. Edmonds who are still in business on the industrial estate.

48 It took me a long time to trace 'A. Milton'. It turned out to be the pharmacy of Julius Hamilton which was in East Street in 1900.

49   The Market Place at the turn of the century with a brewery waggon on the left and a load of hay for someone on the right, outside the Town Hall.

50 The Blandford Choral Society's programme for the 1900 production of *Princess Ida*. Members of the D'Oyly family supported the society and lived in the district.

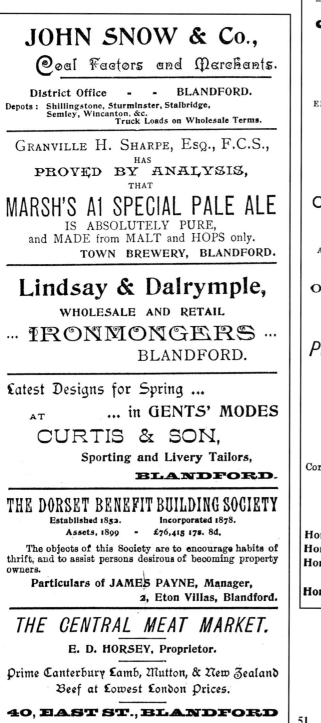

51 Advertisements from the Choral Society's programme of 1900.

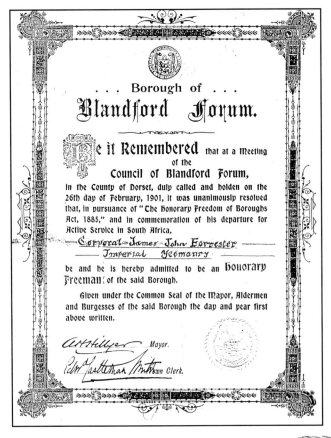

52 Freedom certificate of 1901. These were issued to all Blandford men serving in the Boer War. Corporal James John Forrester served with Paget's Horse and was killed on 13 March 1901.

53 The Blandford family carried on business at 29 Salisbury Street for very many years. This photograph dates from about 1905.

54 Children playing in West Street, with the *Crown Hotel* in the background, *c*.1905.

55 Civic procession marching down Salisbury Street during the 1901 Coronation celebrations.

56 The rear of Blandford's former Milton Abbey Grammar School in East Street *c.*1928, at the time when most of it was demolished. This is now 'Gateways' car park.

57 Blandford residents dressed up for one of the many events which took place in 1905-6 to mark the 300th anniversary of Blandford receiving its Royal Charter of Incorporation in November 1605.

58 The Mayor and Mayoress of Blandford, Mr. and Mrs. John Iles Barnes, arrive for the tercentenary parade via White Cliff Mill Street.

59 The old post office in West Street dressed up for the tercentenary celebrations in 1906.

60 Looking over Blandford bridge from the entrance to Lord Portman's estate *c*.1905. Note the thatched barn in the Marsh.

61 Salisbury Street, *c*.1910. The shop on the left with the large hanging lamp was Hobbs & Co., who have only recently closed their retail shop here.

62 Blandford Rangers footballers, 1908-9, photographed outside the cottage hospital adjoining the recreation ground.

63 The Blandford Gymnastic Club photographed in the 1910-11 season. The club had the use of the Milton Abbey Grammar School gymnasium. Many of their displays were performed to music provided by Miss Peacock (sitting in the middle of the front row).

64 Blandford's female lodge of Oddfellows in the float entered by them for the town's carnival *c.*1915. The building behind is thought to be Marsh's brewery.

65 Fields Oak, off Salisbury Street, one of the town's finest Victorian buildings. It was built by Thomas Hodges Bennett in 1856 and was once occupied by the Woodhouse family who gave part of their garden to the town to become the Woodhouse Gardens. The house was demolished in 1970 and replaced by a new housing estate.

66 Munster House in East Street. This is one of the few houses spoilt by development. The central doorway is now the entrance to Tabernacle Walk and the lower rooms to the left became a shop.

67 Park House at the west end of Bryanston Street was of early 19th-century construction. For most of its time it was occupied by the Hobbs family. It was demolished in recent years to make way for housing.

68 The northern end of White Cliff Mill Street about 1910, with the recreation ground in the distance.

69 Eagle House in White Cliff Mill Street at the turn of the century. The house has recently been restored to become a doctors' surgery and the garden is now a car park in Eagle House gardens.

70 Billhead of Alexander & Cherry, the old-established department store in Salisbury Street, in 1910.

71 A 1916 view of East Street with the Milton Abbey School on the left and the substantial merchant's residence on the right, which was at one time occupied by the Barnes family who were local woolstaplers.

72 Looking down West Street from the Market Place *c.*1910 with the *Crown Hotel* in the distance.

73 The bridges at Blandford seen from Blandford St Mary, *c*.1908. As ever there were plenty of boys out fishing.

JOHN ❋ RIGGS,

THE SUPPLY STORES,

37 & 39, Salisbury St.,

BLANDFORD.

BUY YOUR CHEESE

AT THE

CHEAPEST STORES.

Fine Blue Dorset,

Fresh from the Dairies,

3d.   3½d.   4d.   lb.

Fine Best Cheese 5d. 5½d.

Fine Dry Bacon 3½d. 4d.

Smoked   ,,   from 5d.

Hams from 3½d.

Fine Margarine 4d. 6d.

74 John Riggs was in business at this address from the 1880s until *c.*1915.

75 The western end of East Street showing the sign of the *Star Inn* on the left, a donkey cart and, on the right, the church *c.*1910. There was no footpath below the church railings in those days.

76 Looking up Salisbury Street *c.*1910. This picture was taken from Hobbs' premises.

77 Looking down Salisbury Street *c*.1910. By this time the former Express newspaper office had become a temperance hotel and the Church House was used by the parish for educational and social events.

78 The parish church of St Peter and St Paul during the First World War, with Ashford's shop where the bank is now and a group of soldiers outside the fire memorial.

79 A cartoon relating to the borough council elections of 1908. The participants were all identifiable at the time by the articles being carried. The first three past the post were elected.

80 Some yeomanry men off duty at Blandford camp *c*.1911. They were not Dorset yeomanry. Several yeomanry regiments had their annual camps here, including troops from Hampshire, Wiltshire and elsewhere.

81 The yeomanry camp at Blandford, *c*.1911. The horses seem to be having their nosebags.

82 Tilling Stevens lorries working from Blandford railway station to the camp during the period 1914-18.

83 Wareham & Arscott's delivery cart at Blandford camp during the First World War. Their main business premises were in Salisbury Street, Blandford.

84 The Blandford detachment of Red Cross volunteers (V.A.D.) on parade in Blandford Market Place, *c.*1914. Their commanding officer was Dr. Spooner of Blandford.

85 King George V and Winston Churchill arrive at Blandford in 1916 to inspect the Royal Naval Division stationed at Blandford camp.

86 The rough draft of Rupert Brooke's famous poem *The Soldier* written on officers' mess notepaper at Blandford camp in 1914.

HOOD BATTALION,
2nd NAVAL BRIGADE,
BLANDFORD,
DORSET.

If I should die, think only this of me:
  That there's some corner of a foreign field
That is for ever England. There shall be
  In that rich earth a richer dust concealed;
A dust whom England bore, shaped, made aware,
  Gave once her flowers to love, her ways to roam,
A body of England's, breathing English air,
  Washed by the rivers, blest by suns of home.

And think, this heart, all evil shed away,
  A pulse in the eternal mind, no less
    Gives somewhere back the thoughts by England given,
Her sights and sounds; dreams happy as her day,
  And laughter, learnt of friends; and gentleness,
    In hearts at peace, under an English heaven

RUPERT BROOKE
1887–1915
IF I SHOULD DIE, THINK ONLY THIS OF ME :
THAT THERE'S SOME CORNER OF A FOREIGN FIELD
THAT IS FOREVER ENGLAND. THERE SHALL BE
IN THAT RICH EARTH A RICHER DUST CONCEALED ;
A DUST WHOM ENGLAND BORE, SHAPED, MADE AWARE,
GAVE ONCE, HER FLOWERS TO LOVE, HER WAYS TO ROAM,
A BODY OF ENGLAND'S, BREATHING ENGLISH AIR,
WASHED BY HER RIVERS, BLEST BY SUNS OF HOME.
AND THINK, THIS HEART, ALL EVIL SHED AWAY,
A PULSE IN THE ETERNAL MIND, NO LESS GIVEN;
GIVES SOMEWHERE BACK THE THOUGHTS BY ENGLAND
HER SIGHTS & SOUNDS; DREAMS HAPPY AS HER DAY;
AND LAUGHTER, LEARNT OF FRIENDS; & GENTLENESS,
IN HEARTS AT PEACE, UNDER AN ENGLISH HEAVEN.

87 Rupert Brooke, famous poet, who was stationed at Blandford camp in 1914 with the Royal Naval Division. This memorial to him is in Rugby School where his father had been housemaster.

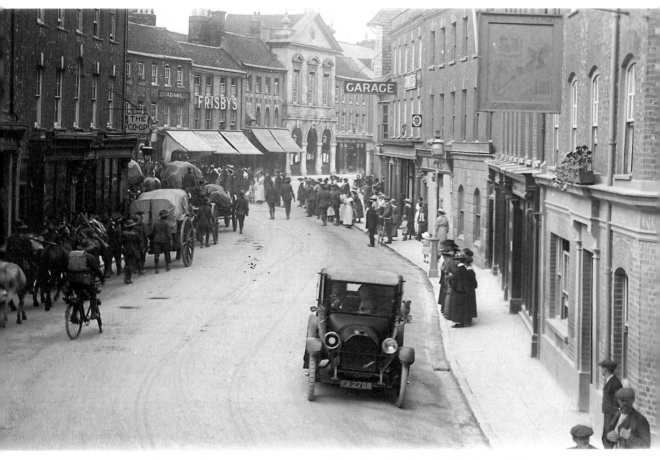

88 Australian troops passing along West Street in Blandford in June 1917.

89 Jack Counter, Blandford's only V.C. from the First World War. He died in Blandford in September 1970 during a return visit from Jersey where he had lived most of his life. His V.C. was awarded for gallantry in France on 16 May 1918 when he carried vital messages under heavy fire after five of his comrades had been killed in the attempt.

90 Town Hall reception for Jack Counter on his return to Blandford in 1918. J.J. Lamperd was mayor at the time.

91   The 1919 Welcome Home celebrations at Blandford in honour of those soldiers, sailors and airmen who returned.

92 Service of Thanksgiving for the end of the war, held in the Market Place.

93 Souvenir postcard of the Y.M.C.A. at Blandford camp, 1916.

94 This 1923 photograph is the only known one of the branch railway which ran from Blandford station to Blandford camp. Soon after it was taken, the line was removed and the cutting used as a dump for Blandford's rubbish. It follows the line of Langton Crescent with Hall & Woodhouse's brewery chimney in the distance. (Picture courtesy of the British Geological Survey.)

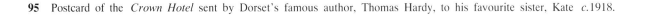

Valentine's Series

POST CARD.

FAMOUS THROUGHOUT THE WORLD

Address Only.

Correspondence

Printed in Great Britain.

GSWA 86

Crown Hotel
Blandford.

Friday. Am here with
Mr Lane. We probably think
of motoring to Shaftesbury today — to Dorchester tomorrow.
F. is at Max G.
with Lilian

T.H.

Miss K. Hardy
Talbothays
nr Dorchester.

95 Postcard of the *Crown Hotel* sent by Dorset's famous author, Thomas Hardy, to his favourite sister, Kate *c.*1918.

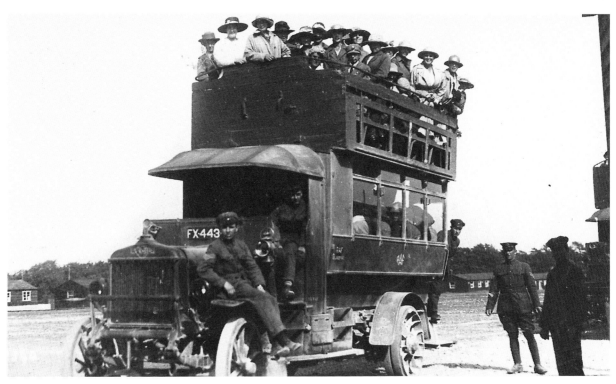

96 The R.A.F. double-decker bus which conveyed passengers to and from the R.A.F. record office at Blandford camp during the period following the end of the First World War.

97 Mr. J.J. Lamperd with his family in their car in 1915. He was mayor of Blandford from 1915-1918.

98 Blandford parish church, from the bottom of Sheep Market hill, *c*.1915.

99 Lord Portman's deer-park, *c.*1916, at Bryanston with the new church of St Martin (sometimes called St Martin's in the fields) in the background.

100 The Second Viscount Portman was a keen huntsman and Master of the Portman Hunt. He died in 1919 but the Portman Hunt is still very active.

1920-1950

101 The Blandford Secondary School in 1920 with war memorial plaques on the gateway. It later became the Blandford Grammar School. The plaques have now been moved to the Blandford School on the Milldown.

102 Blandford Institute Football Club 1920-1. At one time the town had five football clubs playing regularly.

103 East Street at its junction with Damory Street, *c*.1920. The corner shop premises were part of the former union workhouse. Blanchards, solicitors now occupy the building.

104 Upper Salisbury Street with the Ryves Almshouse on the right, *c.*1920.

105 Jay & Sons' shoeing forge in East Street, *c.*1926. William Jay appears on the right of the picture. The sign seen over the door is now in Blandford museum.

Ye OLD MARKET TOWN
Ancient in History, Modern in Commerce. BLANDFORD.

CHARTER OF INCORPORATION IN THE YEAR 1609

BLANDFORD BRIDGES

WHITE CLIFF MILL HILL

BUY IT IN BLANDFORD REMEMBER YOU HAVE DUTIES AS WELL AS RIGHTS. SHOP LOCALLY

BRYANSTON SCHOOL

THE BLANDFORD MARKET PLACE

106 A postcard from the 1920s produced by the Blandford Traders' Association for the benefit of visitors.

107 The Blandford cottage hospital in Picket Close, *c*.1926. It was founded by the Portman family in 1888. Today it is incorporated into the new Blandford community hospital.

108 Blandford St Mary—a peep into the western end of the village from Blandford bridge, *c*.1923.

109 Blandford Market Place in the mid-1920s, with a bull-nosed Morris car on the left and an early village bus in the centre.

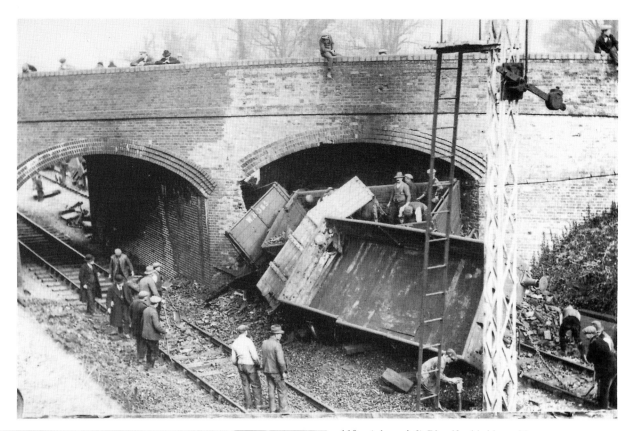

110 (*above left*) Blandford bridge with an oarsman enjoying his exercise and Marsh's Brewery lorry negotiating the bridge, *c.*1925.

111 (*above right*) Train derailment at Blandford St Mary on 6 March 1929 when the early morning train parted company with its waggons.

112 (*left*) The opening of the town's open-air swimming baths in 1924. The baths served the town until 1993.

113 The cottage at the Fairmile, New Road and Dorchester Road junction in 1926. It was demolished in 1960.

114 Blandford post office staff pictured in 1928. At this time the post office was situated in West Street.

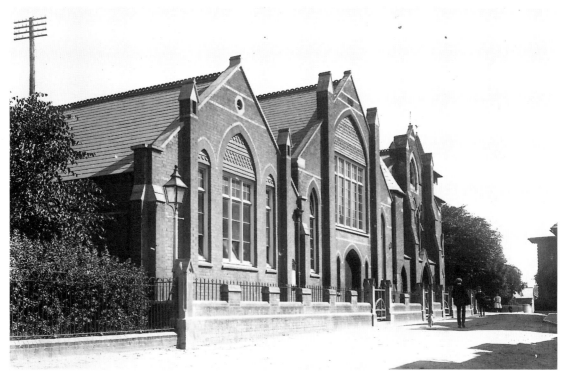

115 The Wesleyan Methodist Chapel in The Close in 1925 complete as finally extended. The front wall and railings no longer exist.

116 The Wesleyan chapel Sunday school outing in 1926.

117 The Palace cinema on the north side of East Street as rebuilt in 1929. It closed in the 1930s when a new Palace opened on the south side of the street. The original Palace reopened after the outbreak of the Second World War, renamed The Ritz.

118 Blandford Cricket Club photographed in Blandford recreation ground, *c.*1925. The young man first left in the front row was Bertie Cecil Hunt, who became an Alderman and Hon. Freeman of the Borough.

119 The visit by the Chief Scout, Sir Robert Baden Powell and Lady Baden Powell to the Blandford Scout and Guide Rally in 1929.

120 The Market Place in the late 1920s. The vehicles helped to date this scene as there has been so little change in the present century.

121 Salisbury Road where it joins Park Road and Damory Street. The *Badger Inn*, established in 1899, can be seen on the left and Mr. Dudderidge's nursery on the right.

122 The borough council and officers in the garden of Fields Oak, the residence of the Mayor, H.S. Woodhouse, in 1926.

123 Mr. L. Bozie's tobacconist's shop, just below the gates to Fields Oak, in Salisbury Street, *c.*1920.

124 Messrs. Sharp & Sons' steam-roller *The Pride of Dorset*. They were roadworks contractors based on the family's St Leonards Farm.

125 The cattle-pens at Blandford railway station, *c*.1928.

126 Railway station staff at Blandford, *c*.1930.

127   Boys of the National School in Blandford, 1930. It is now the Archbishop Wake first school.

128 (*right*) The Rev. H.O. Parnell MA and his Blandford girls' confirmation class and teachers in the early 1930s. He was rector of Blandford from 1929 to 1935.

129 (*below*) Blandford United Football Club, *c*.1933, pictured with Miss Castleman-Smith, Blandford's first lady mayor.

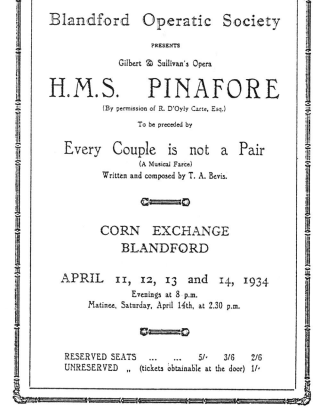

130 (*right*) Programme for Blandford Operatic Society's *HMS Pinafore*, April 1934.

131 Members of the Ancient Order of Buffaloes, Blandford Lodge, *c.*1934. This was an old-established friendly society. It still exists but there is no branch in Blandford now.

132 Blandford Bluecoat schoolboy with pet, *c.*1930. The school closed in 1939 because the boys did not like the distinctive clothing and many parents objected to their boys being called 'charity boys'.

133 Alan Cobham (1894-1980), the aviator who was famous for his 'Flying Circus' and air displays. He was the pioneer of flight refuelling at the former Tarrant Rushton airfield near Blandford. Alan Cobham Engineering Ltd. still functions on Blandford's industrial estate.

134 Sir Alan Cobham's aeroplane *Spirit of the Air* on one of his visits to Blandford, *c*.1932. The airfield was north of the Salisbury Road cemetery.

135 A glimpse into the Market Place shop of H. Gill & Co. Ltd.

136 No.6 Salisbury Street in the 1930s. This is one of the last of Blandford's 18th-century shop fronts. For many years, Eyers & Kerridge were in business here as watch and clockmakers.

137 Lewis Sprackling's double-decker buses at Blandford Market Place in the late 1930s.

138 The New Palace cinema on the south side of East Street (now Gateways/Somerfield). Photograph by the architect, P. Dyson.

139 Blandford Grammar School's form IV in October 1938. The master was Mr. Chappell.

140 Newly arrived National Service recruits at Blandford camp in 1939. They do not look happy!

141 Blandford's mayor, Mr. J.E. Conyers, participating in the civic procession to the church in 1939.

142 Blandford gas works in Damory Street in 1940. Those who say there were two gasometers were right!

143 The Royal Air Force Spitfire, subscribed for by the people of Blandford in the 1940s and named *Who's a Feard*, the county logo. It was shot down at Gravesend on 23 July 1942.

144 The Scouts' huts in Lord Portman's deer-park in 1940. They were taken over by the Home Guard for their headquarters. Note the Anderson shelters used for storage purposes.

145 A German airman being removed to hospital after his Dornier crashed in 1940 on a farm at Nutford. Among those looking on was Cyril Davis, whose family were the owners.

146 The remains of Blandford's Second World War defence system. Many such remains are still in place about the town. These are located behind the *Crown Hotel*.

147 Aerial photograph looking north and showing the post-war council house development in the Elizabeth Road area. The open fields at the top are now industrial estates.

Post 1950

148 View from Blandford church tower over the Old Rectory, the church rooms, The Tabernacle (formerly Winchester Square) and the public library and post office, *c*.1965.

149 Mrs. Ethel M. Biddulph, Mayor of Blandford, reads the 1952 proclamation of Elizabeth II, outside the Town Hall.

150 Blandford Cinder Track team, known as 'The Bats', *c*.1946. They raced on various tracks in the town and district.

151 Miss Mary Phelps, Blandford's 1951 Carnival Queen, with her retinue.

152 The 1954 Blandford Concert Party known as 'The Footlight Follies'. The concerts continued annually in The Palace cinema until the 1960s.

153 The old Magistrates' bench in Blandford Town Hall. This was the court of the Blandford Petty Sessional Division before it moved to new premises in Salisbury Road.

154 The Council Chamber in the Town Hall, still used by the council.

155 An aerial photograph from the 1950s of the town, from which one can pick out many changes which have since occurred.

156 Blandford Grammar School cricket XI, 1955, with the school sportsmaster, Mr. W.J. Paulley.

157 The carnival fairs were held, for many years, in the Market Place. This picture dates from *c.*1962. The newly-established Georgian Fair Day has re-introduced the rides to the Market Place.

158 Blandford Boys' School speech-day, July 1961, attended by Alderman and Mrs. J.L. Carter, the Mayor and Mayoress.

159 The mayoral procession of 1960 with Mayor Edward G. Riggs preceded by the mace-bearers, Mr. Knight and Mr. Jay.

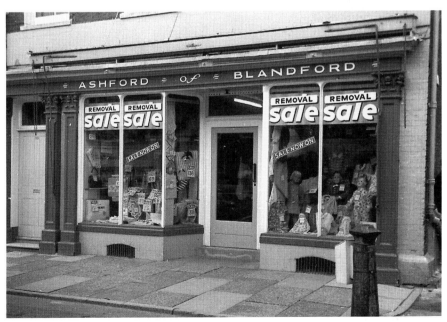

160 The last days of Ashford's, one of Blandford's oldest businesses in the Market Place, taken in 1962. The premises are now part of the National Westminster Bank.

161   Hayward & Coundley's Christmas Market held in the Greyhound Yard, 1961.

162 Pupils of Blandford Infants' School in 1961.

163 Group from Blandford Girls' School (now Archbishop Wake's school) in 1962.

164 The Damory railway arches looking west into the town prior to their destruction in 1978.

165 Engine 40563 with a train for Bournemouth West at Blandford, 11 April 1962. (Courtesy of Joanes Publications.)

166 Engine 41243 leaving Blandford for Bournemouth, 18 June 1963. (Courtesy of Douglas E. Capewell.)

167 Looking down from the old railway embankment onto Damory Court Street after the closure of the line.

168 The last days of Blandford railway station in the late 1960s.

169 The Damory railway bridges looking west and 'going west' on 25 July 1978, as they had become a traffic hazard and were getting into a dangerous structural condition.

170 Market day at Blandford. A difficult picture to date accurately, it was probably taken in the mid-1960s.

It's
BLANDFORD
for our
Christmas
Shopping

1 FX 68

171 The Chamber of Trade's Christmas shopping advertisement of 1968.

172 Looking down Church Street in 1966 with Coupar House (now Legion House) on the left and Lime Tree House on the right.

173 The Blandford Secondary Modern School, erected in Lord Portman's former deer-park in 1955.

174 The former Damory Street Grammar School moved to premises adjoining the Secondary Modern School on going 'comprehensive' in 1968 and became known as 'The Upper School' and now just Blandford School.

175 The former Grammar School premises in Damory Street in course of demolition in 1972. The school gates have been left intact.

176 East Street at the time of the severe flooding of 1979. The new flood barrier erected by National Rivers Authority will hopefully prevent this scene ever being repeated.

177 No, a bomb did not drop on Chestnut House. This is the rear of the property in the course of redevelopment in 1988. Note the Second World War pill-box in the foreground.

178 General view over the south of the Market Place *c.*1970 showing the extensive properties to the rear of the main street, rarely seen by the public.

Suggested Further Reading

Cox, B.G., *The Book of Blandford* (1984)
Country Life Ltd., *Old Towns Revisited* (1952)
Colvin, H.M., *The Bastards of Blandford* (1948)
Hawkins, D., *Cranborne Chase* (1980)
Hinchy, F.S., *The Heart of Dorset* (1953)
Hutchings, J., *The History and Antiquities of the County of Dorset* (1861-1870)
Insall, D.W. and Associates, *Blandford Forum—Conserve and Enhance* (1970)
Mills, A.D., *The Place Names of Dorset* Part III (1980)
Newman, J. & Pevsner, N., *The Buildings of England (Dorset)* (1972)
Nicolson, A. & Morter, P., *Prospects of England* (1989)
Penn, F.J.K., *Historical Towns in Dorset* (1980)
Smith, P., *Blandford* (1968)
Royal Commission on Historical Monuments, Vol.III, part I (1970)